PRAYING WITH
ST. JOHN PAUL II

PRAYING
WITH
ST. JOHN PAUL II

By
Jean-Yves Garneau

Translated from the French by
Rev. Msgr. C. Anthony Ziccardi, S.S.L., S.T.D.

CATHOLIC BOOK PUBLISHING CORP.
New Jersey

NIHIL OBSTAT:
Rev. Msgr. James M. Cafone, M.A., S.T.D.
Censor Librorum

IMPRIMATUR:
✠ Most Rev. John J. Myers, J.C.D., D.D.
Archbishop of Newark

This book was originally published in French by Médiaspaul, 3965 boul. Henri-Bourassa Est, Montréal, QC, H1H 1L1 (Canada), under the title *Nouvaine de prières avec le bien heureux Jean-Paul II*.

(T-74)

ISBN 978-1-937913-95-3

© 2014 by *Catholic Book Publishing Corp.*, NJ
Printed in the U.S.A.
www.catholicbookpublishing.com

CONTENTS

INTRODUCTION

THE word "novena" comes from the Latin *novem* (nine). To make a novena is to undertake an itinerary of prayer that will last nine days and will have as its aim to request from God one or more favors. If possible, the nine days will follow one another without interruption. But one may also make a novena of two days over two days' time or at the rate of one day per week over nine weeks. It is really up to each person to choose the rhythm that is suitable. What is important is to pray persistently, perseveringly, and confidently.

It is difficult to say with certainty what may be the origin of the novena of prayers that has become popular in Catholicism. Several authors relate it to the nine days during which, after Jesus' resurrection, the disciples remained in prayer with Mary. Here is what is written in the Acts of the Apostles:

While at table with [his apostles], Jesus enjoined them not to depart from Jerusalem, but to wait for "the promise of the Father about which you have heard me speak; for John baptized with water, but in a few days you will be baptized with the Holy Spirit." ... Then from the Mount of Olives they returned to Jerusalem. . . . When they entered the city they went to the upper room where they were staying, Peter and John and James and Andrew, Philip and Thomas, Bartholomew and Matthew, James son of Alphaeus, Simon the Zealot, and Judas son of James. All, with one accord, devoted themselves to prayer, together with some women, and Mary the mother of Jesus, and his brothers *(Acts 1:4-5, 12-14)*.

During this novena, we will have nine specific requests to make of God in union with Saint John Paul II and through his intercession.

Day One: Lord, let me love life.

Day Two: Lord, give me the joy of believing.

Day Three: Lord, grant me to know your will.

Day Four: Lord, fill me with the spirit of strength.

Day Five: Lord, protect families.

Day Six: Lord, help me to carry my cross.

Day Seven: Lord, teach me to pray to you.

Day Eight: Lord, teach me to love.

Day Nine: Lord, teach me to forgive.

For each day of the novena, the following course is proposed:

1. *I make the Sign of the Cross, and I ask God to help me to pray.*
2. *I think about John Paul II.*
3. *I read some verses from the New Testament.*
4. *I reflect on what I have just read.*
5. *I read some lines penned by John Paul II.*
6. *I pray for myself.*
7. *I present to God various personal prayer intentions.*

8. *I pray for the Church and for all who live on earth.*

9. *I recite an* Our Father, *a* Hail Mary *and a* Glory be.

LORD, LET ME LOVE LIFE

1. *I slowly make the Sign of the Cross while saying:* In the name of the Father, and of the Son, and of the Holy Spirit.

Then I say: Gracious God, help me to pray to You well with Saint John Paul II.

2. *I think about John Paul II:*

He loved life, and he lived with intensity every phase of it. He did not retreat in face of difficulties, and he never hesitated to take up challenges. He fulfilled his responsibilities as Pope to the utmost degree. What does this man mean to me? If I were asked to point to one thing that has especially struck me about him, what would my response be?

3. *I read some verses from the New Testament:*

- [It is written:] "I am the God of Abraham, the God of Isaac, and the God of Jacob." He is God, not of the dead, but of the living *(Mk 12:26-27)*.

- I came so that they might have life and have it more abundantly *(Jn 10:10)*.

- The Son of Man came not to be served but to serve, and to give his life as a ransom for many *(Mt 20:28)*.

- I am the resurrection and the life; whoever believes in me, even if he dies, will live, and whoever lives and believes in me will never die *(Jn 11:25-26)*.

- Whoever wants to save his life will lose it; but anyone who loses his life for my sake, and for the sake of the gospel, will save it *(Mk 8:35)*.

- Eternal life is that they should know you, the only true God, and the one whom you sent, Jesus Christ *(Jn 17:3)*.

4. *I reflect on what I have just read:*

Human life is very precious. Do I appreciate its value?

Life with God is also very precious. Baptism has made me a creature entirely united to God, one of His children in the bosom of the Church. Do I appreciate this enough to give thanks?

I cannot explain how, according to His promise, Jesus Christ transmits His life to me, but I am certain that this is so. My faith assures me of it. I believe that Jesus is for me "the Way and the Truth and the Life" *(Jn 14:6)*.

To live well and in harmony with the Gospel is not to seek to grab everything for oneself, to desire the first place, to be praised constantly, to be served by everyone. . . . Rather, it is to accept one's place with joy and humility, to put oneself at the service of others, to be attentive to their needs, and to know how to forget oneself for their sake.

The one who lives only for himself destroys his life. The one who knows how to put his life at others' service lives fully. Such a person lives as a disciple of Jesus; indeed, he draws his life from God's own life.

If these thoughts induce me to reflection, I re-read one or another of them; otherwise, I re-read the New Testament texts that I read previously.

5. *I read some lines penned by John Paul II:*

Whether it be long or short, life is a voyage to paradise: there is our homeland and our true home; there we have an appointment with Someone!

Jesus waits for us in paradise! Never forget this supreme and consoling truth. (*Discourse to Children*, given on the occasion of their First Holy Communion, at the Vatican on June 14, 1979.)

The gift of life which God the Creator and Father has entrusted to man calls him to appreciate the inestimable value of what he has been given and to take responsibility for it. (Encyclical Letter *Donum vitæ*, February 22, 1987, no. 1.)

In the light of the truth about the gift of human life and in the light of the moral principles which flow from that truth, everyone is invited to act in the area of responsibility proper to each, and, like the Good Samaritan, to recognize as a neighbor even the littlest among the children of men *(see Lk 10:29-37)*. Here Christ's word finds a new and particular echo: "What you do to one of the least of my brethren, you do unto me" *(Mt 25:40)*. (Encyclical Letter *Donum vitæ*, Conclusion.)

6. *I thank God as I say over and over:*

Thank you, Lord, for my life and the life of the persons whom I love and who love me.

Then I implore Him more than once, saying:

Lord, let me love life.
Lord, let Your life grow in me, and let it grow also in those who love me and in those whom I love.

7. *With Saint John Paul II and by his intercession, I present to God my personal intentions. I name the persons for whom I pray, and I tell God what I request of Him for them.*

8. *I pray for the Church and for all who live on earth:*

• That respect may be accorded to every life which is born or grows or is approaching its end, I pray to You, Lord.

- That the Holy Spirit may give the active members of the Church the courage to announce joyously that Christ has passed beyond death and that He is forever the Source of life, I present my prayer, all-good God.

- For all those who do not know Jesus Christ, that they may discover Him to be "the Way, the Truth, and the Life," I call upon You, Lord.

- That those who are tempted to take their own lives may be found and helped, I ask You with fervor, God of life.

- That throughout the world the life of plants and watercourses and animals and forests may be increasingly respected, I raise my prayer to You, Lord.

- That the Christian life transmitted to young people at their Baptism may increase and grow, I ask and implore You, Lord.

- That those who are nourished on the bread of the Eucharist may grow in faith and hope and love, I beseech

You, Lord, from the bottom of my heart.

9. *I recite an* Our Father, *a* Hail Mary *and a* Glory be.

Our Father

OUR Father, who art in heaven,
hallowed be thy name;
thy kingdom come,
thy will be done
on earth as it is in heaven.
Give us this day our daily bread,
and forgive us our trespasses,
as we forgive those who trespass
against us;
and lead us not into temptation,
but deliver us from evil.
Amen.

Hail Mary

HAIL Mary,
full of grace,
the Lord is with you.
Blessed are you among women
and blessed is the fruit of your womb,
Jesus.

Holy Mary,
Mother of God,
pray for us sinners,
now and at the hour of our death.
Amen.

Glory Be

G LORY be to the Father,
and to the Son,
and to the Holy Spirit.
As it was in the beginning,
is now, and ever shall be,
world without end.
Amen.

LORD, GIVE ME THE JOY OF BELIEVING

1. *I slowly make the Sign of the Cross while saying:* In the name of the Father, and of the Son, and of the Holy Spirit.

Then I say: Gracious God, help me to pray to You well with Saint John Paul II.

2. *I think about John Paul II:*

I call to mind some photographs of him before he became seriously ill. The majority of these pictures show him smiling and sometimes laughing heartily.

The more one is familiar with this man the more one knows that, despite the difficulties he faced and the sufferings he endured, he was a Christian, a priest, a bishop, a cardinal, and a Pope who was happy to believe.

3. *I read some verses from the New Testament:*

- Jesus said to Thomas: "You believe because you see me. Blessed are those who have not seen and yet have believed" *(Jn 20:29)*.

- Everything is possible to him who believes *(Mk 9:23)*.

- Truly, truly, I say to you, whoever believes in me will also do the works that I do, and will do greater ones than these, because I go to the Father *(Jn 14:12)*.

- Day after day, with one heart, [the believers] went to the Temple and met in their homes for the breaking of the bread; they took their meals gladly and generously; they praised God and enjoyed favor with all the people *(Acts 2:46-47)*.

- Blessed are you when people insult you and persecute you and speak all kinds of calumny against you on my account. Rejoice and be glad, for your reward will be great in heaven *(Mt 5:11-12)*.

- Rejoice always. Pray without ceasing. In all circumstances give thanks. This is the will of God for you in Christ Jesus *(1 Thes 5:16-18)*.

- I am overflowing with joy in all our hardships *(2 Cor 7:4)*.

4. *I read some lines penned by John Paul II:*

> *Christ certainly desires faith.* He desires it *from human beings* and he desires it *for* human beings. To those seeking miracles from Him He used to respond: "Your faith has saved you" *(see Mk 10:52)*. The case of the Canaanite woman is especially striking. At first it appears as though Jesus does not want to listen to her request that He help her daughter, almost as if He wanted to move her to the stirring profession of faith, "But even the dogs eat the scraps that fall from their masters' table" *(Mt 15:27)*. He puts the foreign woman to the test, in order then to be able to say: "Great is your faith. Let it be done for you as you desire" *(Mt 15:28)*.

Jesus wants to rouse faith in human beings. He desires that we respond to the word of the Father, but He simulta-nously wants to respect human dignity. For in the search itself for faith, a kind of faith is already present, an implicit faith, and therefore the necessary condition for salvation is already met. (*Crossing the Threshold of Hope*, no. 29 ["Of What Use Is Faith?"], 1994.)

5. *I reflect on what I have just read:*

Faith is a gift. Some people receive it a few days after their birth, at the time of their Baptism. Others do not receive it until later. In either case, faith is a gift that, at some moment or other, needs to be accepted. Faith is imposed on no one. But it is offered widely, throughout the earth.

When anyone becomes aware of the gift of faith that he has been given, he becomes responsible for consenting to it, for cultivating it, for protecting it, and for making it increase. Still, the faith that was welcomed today may be set aside or ignored tomorrow.

Does my faith increase from year to year? What could I do to help it increase?

Faith is never a burden to be carried on one's shoulders. Rather, it should, at all times and in all circumstances, be a reason for joy . . . a joy wholly interior: the joy of knowing ourselves to be loved by God, the joy of being sure that He will never withdraw His love from us, the joy of being convinced that on our most difficult days the Lord does not cease to accompany us and support us.

All the Saints—frequently in the midst of great suffering—have been able to make their own the words of the Apostle Paul: "I rejoice in the sufferings I endure for your sake" *(Col 1:24)*.

What makes us happy in every situation is knowing that we are loved. God's love for us does not fail.

6. *I thank God as I say over and over:*

Thank You, Lord, for the faith You have given me.

Then I implore Him more than once, saying:

Increase my faith, Lord. Make it fervent and joyous.

7. *With Saint John Paul II and by his intercession, I present to God my personal intentions. I name the persons for whom I pray, and I tell God what I request of Him for them.*

8. *I pray for the Church and for all who live on earth:*

- Lord, go to meet those who search for You.

- Enlighten those who doubt Your existence.

- Touch the hearts of those who no longer believe in You.

- Draw close to You those who formerly loved You but now are far from You.

- Support those who aspire to the life of perfection.

- I pray to You now for the Pope and the bishops: that their faith may be firm and joyful.

- I pray to You for all parents who will educate their children in the faith: that they may do it with love and patience, and not only with words, but with the whole of their lives.

- I pray to You for all pastoral ministers: that they may be skilled at leading to You all whom they meet.

- I pray to You for young Christians: that they may have the courage not to blush on account of their faith in the company of their friends.

- Lord, give the joy of believing to all disciples of Jesus.

- Give it to those who are undergoing severe trials.

- Give it to those who are preparing themselves for Baptism.

- Give it to all missionaries who announce the Gospel in faraway places.

9. *I recite an* Our Father, *a* Hail Mary, *and a* Glory be.

LORD, GRANT ME TO KNOW YOUR WILL

1. *I slowly make the Sign of the Cross while saying:* In the name of the Father, and of the Son, and of the Holy Spirit.

Then I say: Gracious God, help me to pray to You well with Saint John Paul II.

2. *I think about John Paul II:*

Often during his life, he had to make important decisions: to become a priest and then to accept being made a bishop and then a cardinal and Pope.

Very often he must have asked himself: Should I speak or should I be silent? Should I take this initiative or not? Should I speak up about this or that subject, while knowing that some people will not appreciate what I have to say?

He would make his decisions after having prayed much and after having weighed the pros and cons of the issues upon which he would speak publicly.

His decisions were the result of a prior search for God's will.

3. *I read some verses from the New Testament:*

- [Jesus said to the rich, young man who questioned him:] "If you want to be perfect, go and sell what you possess and give it to the poor, and you will have treasure in heaven; then come, follow me" *(Mt 9:21)*.

- Father, if you are willing, take this cup away from me; nevertheless, not my will but yours be done *(Lk 22:42)*.

- Do not model your behavior on the present world, but let the renewing of your minds transform you, so that you yourselves may discern what is the will of God—what is good, pleasing to him, and perfect *(Rom 12:2)*.

- Whoever does the will of my Father in heaven is my brother and sister and mother *(Mt 12:50)*.

- The world with its enticements is passing away. But whoever does the will of God remains forever *(1 Jn 2:17)*.

4. *I read some lines penned by John Paul II:*

In the Garden of Olives, facing His Passion and Cross, Jesus grasps the full scope of evil in the human heart and history, and He asks that "this cup" be taken from Him; regardless, He says: "Father, not my will, but your will." This is why this prayer is so poignant a moment in the whole of His mission. This is the moment to which return ceaselessly our questions concerning evil in the world as permitted and accepted by the eternal plan of God . . . of the Father. . . . (*Mon livre de méditations, Éditions du Rocher*, 2004, no. 431, p. 150.)

5. *I reflect on what I have just read:*

It is not always easy to know God's will. In order to come to it, it is necessary to reflect, to keep silent, to explore Jesus' words, and to invoke the Holy Spirit. Occasionally, it is good to let ourselves be helped by an advisor in order to discover what God desires of us. Many months and years may pass before we see clearly that to which God is calling us.

God asks of us all kinds of things: those that are easy to accomplish, those that are less easy, those that are difficult, and those that are very difficult.

Jesus said unequivocally that to follow Him on the way to the Father it would be necessary to take up the cross.

No one loves the cross. Often, we find that ours is not the one that suits us. We prefer to select our own cross!

Jesus did not choose His own Cross. He agreed to shoulder the one that the Father wanted to see Him carry.

When God demands much from us, we should recall that He never requires of us what is beyond our abilities and that He Himself gives us the strength to do what He asks.

6. *I thank God as I think of some trials that I have endured. I say to Him over and over:*

Thanks be to You, Lord, for having been close to me. Thank You for supporting me.

Then I implore Him more than once, saying:

Lord, let me know what You expect of me each day.
Grant me to love Your will.
And give me the courage to accomplish it.

7. *With Saint John Paul II and by his intercession, I present to God my personal intentions. I name the persons for whom I pray, and I tell God what I request of Him for them.*

8. *I pray for the Church and for all who live on earth:*

• Lord God, let the Church act according to Your will.

• Let the Church announce the Gospel without distortion.

• Let the Church dare to summon the baptized to heroism and sanctity.

• Let the Church live in truth and transparency.

- Let all the members of the Church help one another to live in faith, hope, and love.

- Lord Jesus, support all Christian parents who strive to give their children a Christian education.

- Support our young people's educators in the faith.

- Support Christians who are persecuted or whose life is threatened because of their faith.

- Support those who have a heavy cross; carry it with them.

- Lord God, send Your Spirit down upon us: may He be our light and our strength; may He keep us in joy, peace, faithfulness, and love.

9. *I recite an* Our Father, *a* Hail Mary, *and a* Glory be.

LORD, FILL ME WITH THE SPIRIT OF STRENGTH

1. *I slowly make the Sign of the Cross while saying:* In the name of the Father, and of the Son, and of the Holy Spirit.

Then I say: Gracious God, help me to pray to You well with Saint John Paul II.

2. *I think about John Paul II:*

From the day that he became Pope, he seemed to everyone to be self-possessed, solid, and capable of issuing great challenges. His faith was strong and radiant. Far from placing it under a bushel, he proclaimed it with gusto. He neither hid nor downplayed the disturbing or demanding parts of the Gospel. He did not speak or act to please those who had their eyes on him. He was conscious of what God expected of him.

Throughout the years, he opposed energetically the powers of communism. He remained true to himself

when he succeeded John Paul I. It is
no surprise that during his first speech
he made his own the words that Jesus
addressed to His disciples: "Do not be
afraid!"

3. *I read some verses from the Gospel
    of Matthew:*

• Do not be afraid of those who kill the
   body but cannot kill the soul; fear him
   rather who can destroy both body
   and soul in Gehenna. Are not two
   sparrows sold for a small coin? And
   yet not one falls to the ground without your Father's knowledge. Every
   hair on your head has been num-
   bered! Therefore, there is no need to
   be afraid; you are worth more than a
   flock of sparrows. If anyone declares
   himself for me in the presence of
   human beings, I will declare myself
   for him in the presence of my Father
   in heaven *(Mt 10:28-32).*

• When the disciples saw Jesus walk-
   ing on the sea, they were terrified. "It
   is a ghost," they said, crying out in
   fear. But at once Jesus said to them,

"Take courage! It is I! Do not be afraid" *(Mt 14:26-27)*.

- [On the mountain where Jesus was transfigured] a voice came from the cloud, saying: "This is my beloved Son, who enjoys my favor. Listen to him." When they heard this, the disciples fell on their faces, overcome with fear. But Jesus came up and touched them, saying, "Stand up. Do not be afraid" *(Mt 17:5-7)*.

4. *I reflect on what I have just read:*

Let us never pretend to be without fear. There exist instinctive fears: fear at the moment of an accident, fear of being hurt by a person who threatens us, fear of losing someone we love, fear of falling short of being what we would want to be. . . . Nonetheless, let us push ourselves to master our fears. Often it is possible.

Helpful in overcoming fear is having near us a person in whom we put our total trust. It is very helpful to hold the hand of someone whom we love and who loves us in turn.

Jesus invited His disciples to over-
come their fear by thinking about God.
He is your providence, according to
Jesus' teaching, and your life rests in
His attentive hands.

Even if all our friends abandon us—
may God never allow this for us—God
Himself will always be at our side. He
was at Jesus' side when He (Jesus)
called out to Him from the Cross: "My
God, my God, why have your abandoned me?" *(Mt 27:46).*

5. *I read some lines penned by John
   Paul II:*

On October 22, 1978, when I spoke
the words "Do not be afraid!" in St.
Peter's Square, I could not have realized just how far they would take me
and the Church as a whole. Their con-
tent came more from the Holy Spirit,
promised by the Lord Jesus to His disciples as the Consoler, than from the
man who mouthed them. . . .

The exhortation "Do not be afraid!"
should be interpreted broadly. In a
certain sense, *it was an exhortation ad-*

dressed to all human beings, an exhortation to overcome fear in the current state of the world, as much in the East as in the West, as much in the North as in the South.

Do not be afraid of that which you yourselves have created. Do not be afraid of all that human beings have made and that every day is becoming more of a danger to them! Do not be afraid of yourselves!

Why should we not fear? Because man has been redeemed by God. . . . "Fear not!": "For God so loved the world that he gave his only Son" *(cf. Jn 3:16).* . . . [Christ] is the light that "shines in the darkness, and the darkness has not overcome it" *(cf. Jn 1:5).* (*Crossing the Threshold of Hope*, no. 34 ["So as Not to Be Afraid"], 1994.)

6. *I thank God as I say over and over:*

I thank You, Lord, for Your constant presence in my life.

Then I implore Him more than once, saying:

Lord, give me the strength to bear witness to my faith with courage.

7. *With Saint John Paul II and by his intercession, I present to God my personal intentions. I name the persons for whom I pray, and I tell God what I request of Him for them.*

8. *I pray for the Church and for all who live on earth:*

- With Saint John Paul II, I pray to You, Lord, for those who at school or in college risk being ridiculed for declaring themselves to be practicing Christians: give them the courage to expound firmly their convictions.

- I pray to You for Christians who are persecuted in various countries: that numerous may be the persons and organizations that step forward to defend them.

- I pray to You for all those who on occasion are afraid of You because they have behaved badly or because they have not known You well:

grant them to see that You are the God Who loves and forgives.

- I pray to You for all in the Church who are frequently tempted to hold on to the past rather than forge ahead into the future: let them see that the Spirit calls the Church to constant renewal.

- I pray to You for those who are responsible for the Church: give them light and courage and strength to undertake necessary reforms so that evangelization might be pursued with zest and bear greater fruit.

- I pray to You for the dying: that they may wrap up their lives while offering themselves to You and being assured that they are coming to meet You.

9. *I recite an* Our Father, *a* Hail Mary, *and a* Glory be.

LORD, PROTECT FAMILIES

1. *I slowly make the Sign of the Cross while saying:* In the name of the Father, and of the Son, and of the Holy Spirit.

   Then I say: Gracious God, help me to pray to You well with Saint John Paul II.

2. *I think about John Paul II:*

   Born on May 18, 1920, he received at his Baptism the name of Karol Jósef Wojtyla.

   Olga, his sister, whom he never knew, died at birth in 1914.

   He lost his mother, Emilia Kaszorowska, in 1929.

   His older brother, Edmond, who was a physician, died in 1932.

   His father, Karol Wojtyla, died on February 16, 1941.

3. *I read some verses from the Bible:*

   - Whoever respects his father will be gladdened by children; on the day he prays for help, he will be heard. Long life comes to anyone who honors his father; whoever obeys the Lord gives comfort to his mother. Such a person serves his parents as well as the Lord. Respect your father in deed as well as word, so that blessing may come on you from him. . . . Support your father in his old age; do not grieve him during his life. Even if his mind should fail, show him kindness; do not despise him in your health and strength. For kindness to a father will not be forgotten. . . . In your time of trial, God will remember you *(Sir 3:5-8, 12-15)*.

• Be clothed in heartfelt compassion, generosity, humility, gentleness, and patience. Bear with one another and forgive each other. . . . And over all these, put on love, the perfect bond. And may the peace of Christ reign in your hearts *(Col 3:12-15)*.

• [After a three-day search, Jesus' parents find Him in the Temple in the company of teachers.] His mother said to him, "My child, why have you done this to us? See how worried your father and I have been, looking for you." He replied, "Why were you looking for me? Did you not know that I must be in my Father's house?" But they did not understand what he meant *(Lk 2:48-50).*

4. *I reflect on what I have just read:*

What is received in the bosom of the family is a treasure that endures for life.

It is in the family that we learn to live with others, to show mutual respect, to love one another, to help each other, and to forgive one another. There is no better place than the family to learn to become an adult worthy of the name.

Like most of us, Jesus received much from His family: a language, a culture, a tradition, the knowledge and love of the God of Israel. His parents had a decisive influence on Him.

It is quite normal that in families there be misunderstandings and conflicts. Such were present in Jesus' family. As all families, His family was a place of happiness and of suffering. But it was, above all, a place in which love was never lacking.

Three things are especially important to preserving family life: getting together, communicating with one another, and forgiving each other. Do I do this as much as possible in my family?

5. *I read some lines penned by John Paul II:*

In order that the family may be, as Chesterton affirmed, "a cell of resistance to oppression," it must be a community of great maturity and profundity. When I say "it must," I mean that this is a moral obligation. To speak of the family as "a cell of resistance to oppression" is to indicate its moral value and, simultaneously, to specify the structure that is proper to it; and, in the final analysis, it is to assume as foundational the spiritual maturity of persons. (*Homily*, given in Warsaw on June 2, 1979; *Mon livre de méditations*, Éditions du Rocher, 2004, no. 82, p. 36.)

The family constitutes the most realized community as regards human relationships. There is no relationship uniting persons more strongly than the marital and familial bond. There is no other tie that could be defined so fully a "communion." There is no other wherein the mutual obligations are so deep and complete, so that any attack on them injures painfully human sensibility: that of men, of women, of children, of parents. (*Homily*, given in Maslowo on June 3, 1979; *Mon livre de méditations*, Éditions du Rocher, 2004, no. 83, p. 36.)

6. *I thank God as I say over and over:*

I give You thanks, Lord, for all that I have received in the bosom of my family.

Then I think of my father, my mother, and all that they have passed on to me. I pray to God, saying:

I give You thanks for all that I have received from my mother.

I give You thanks for all that I have received from my father.

If I have brothers and sisters, I think of them, and I pray especially for them.

7. *With Saint John Paul II and by his intercession, I then present to God other personal intentions of mine for some families that I know. I name the persons for whom I pray, and I tell God what I request of Him for them.*

8. *I pray for the Church and for today's families:*

• I pray to You, Lord, that the whole Church may be a place of fraternity, love, and forgiveness. I implore, You, gracious God, that a family spirit may blossom in my parish (or my community).

• I lift up my prayer to You, Lord, that throughout the earth fathers and mothers of families may succeed at educating their children in liberty, responsibility, and love.

• I pray to You also for divided families, for those families wounded by violence and misunderstanding, for brothers and sisters who no longer speak to one another, for parents who need support but can find none. Come to their help, Lord.

9. *I recite an* Our Father, *a* Hail Mary, *and a* Glory be.

LORD, HELP ME TO CARRY
MY CROSS

1. *I slowly make the Sign of the Cross while saying:* In the name of the Father, and of the Son, and of the Holy Spirit.

Then I say: Gracious God, help me to pray to You well with Saint John Paul II.

2. *I think about John Paul II:*

Like all of us, he had a cross to bear. One thinks here of his childhood and the sorrow he must have known in losing his mother, then his brother, and finally his father.

He had also the cross of his pastoral ministry, always more important, always heavier. For a long time, he exercised his ministry in the face of communist oppression.

One may think also of the crosses, small and large, caused by what others might have said about him or by what he was not able to accomplish despite his best efforts.

And finally there was the cross of his long and agonizing illness.

3. *I read some verses from the New Testament:*

* Becoming as human beings are and being found human in appearance, he was humbler still, even to accepting death, death on a cross. For this God raised him high, and gave him the name which is above all other names *(Phil 2:7-9)*.

* If anyone wants to be a follower of mine, let him renounce himself and take up his cross and follow me *(Mt 16:24)*.

* I consider that the sufferings of this present time are not worth comparing with the glory that is to be revealed in us *(Rom 8:18)*.

* Now I find joy in the sufferings I endure for your sake, and in my flesh I complete what is lacking in Christ's afflictions for the sake of his Body, that is, the Church *(Col 1:24)*.

- Take as examples of hardship and patience, brothers, the prophets who spoke in the name of the Lord *(Jas 5:10)*.

- But if, when you do good, you suffer patiently, this is a grace before God *(1 Pet 2:20)*.

- But insofar as you share in the sufferings of Christ, be joyful, so that when his glory is revealed you may rejoice and be glad *(1 Pet 4:13)*.

4. *I reflect on what I have just read:*

Suffering hurts. We should not seek it out. We should not consider ourselves above it. Jesus prayed that, if possible, the Cross presented to Him might be taken from Him.

It was not possible. Therefore, He accepted it and carried it to the end . . . to His death.

His suffering was real, not feigned. His pains were real; they were physical and psychological and spiritual. An attentive reading of the Gospels reveals that His greatest suffering was to feel abandoned by His Father.

If Jesus was able to keep going to the end, it is because He was confident that His suffering was not in vain. It was the clearest sign of the love that He had for His Father and for those whom the Father had entrusted to Him.

Love always ends up bearing fruit.

Having borne His sufferings, Jesus conquered death and found life again. He is now and forever the Risen One, the Savior of the world.

5. *I read some lines penned by John Paul II:*

Gethsemane and Calvary teach us that the Son of God found Himself in the same situation as every human being struggling in this world with the force of evil. He was on the side of the man who suffers. In this place of agony, He proclaimed to the end the Kingdom of God and the truth of the love that is stronger than passion and stronger than death.

We believe that in taking on Himself the weight of evil He conquered evil, that He conquered sin and death, that

He grafted onto the root of suffering the power of the Redemption and the light of hope. Those who suffer and whom I have been privileged to meet in my pastoral ministry have given me testimony of this and continue to provide it to me daily. (*Mon livre de méditations*, Éditions du Rocher, 204, no. 452, p. 155.)

6. *I thank God as I say over and over:*

By the death of Your Son on the Cross and by His great love, Father, I praise and give You thanks.

Then I implore Him more than once, saying:

Lord Jesus, help me to carry my cross and to do so in love.

7. *With Saint John Paul II and by his intercession, I present to God my personal intentions. I name the persons for whom I pray, and I tell God what I request of Him for them.*

8. *I pray for the Church and for all who live on earth:*

• For all those to whom important roles have been entrusted in the

Church and who find it difficult to implement them.

— Come to their aid, Lord.

• For consecrated persons who live in mortification, silence, prayer, and fraternity.

— Support them every day, Lord.

• For priests discouraged by the immensity of their responsibilities and by the scarce fruit that their efforts seem to produce.

— Encourage them, Lord.

• For parents disappointed by their failure to transmit to their children the values in which they believe and by which they themselves seek to live.

— Come to their rescue, Lord.

• For those wounded by life, by drug abuse, by violence, and by scorn.

— Let them see Your love, Lord.

• For those who foment and practice violence, for people who exploit those who surround them.

— Change their hearts, Lord.

- For those who find too heavy the cross they must bear.

  —That they may know that You carry it with them, Lord.

- Gracious God, welcome with bounteousness these requests and grant them through Jesus Christ, our Lord.

  — Amen.

9. *I recite an* Our Father, *a* Hail Mary, *and a* Glory be.

LORD, TEACH ME TO PRAY
TO YOU

1. *I slowly make the Sign of the Cross while saying:* In the name of the Father, and of the Son, and of the Holy Spirit.

   Then I say: Gracious God, help me to pray to You well with Saint John Paul II.

2. *I think about John Paul II:*

   All who knew him agree with one another that he was a man of prayer. Cardinal Georges Marie Martin Cottier stated that "he made decisions on his knees."

   It is said that he always had a notebook in hand when he was in his private chapel; and during his meditations, he wrote down whatever insights came to him from the Spirit.

   It is reported that every morning his secretary would slip into the bookrack of his kneeler a list of personal requests that came from everywhere. These requests fueled his prayer.

He had a special devotion to Mary, the Mother of God.

3. *I read some verses from the New Testament:*

- Be vigilant and pray at all times for the strength to escape all that is going to happen and to stand before the Son of Man *(Lk 21:36)*.

- When you pray, do not be like the hypocrites: they love to say their prayers standing up in the synagogues and at the street corners for people to see them. . . . As for you, when you pray, go to your room, shut yourself in, and pray to your Father in that secret place, and your Father who sees in secret will reward you *(Mt 6:5-6)*.

- Ask, and it will be given to you; search, and you will find; knock, and the door will be opened to you. . . . If you then, who are wicked, know how to give good things to your children, how much more will your

Father in heaven give good things to those who ask him? *(Mt 7:7, 11)*.

- Pray for your persecutors *(Mt 5:44)*.

- [The members of the first Christian community] devoted themselves to the teaching of the apostles and to the communal life, to the breaking of the bread, and to the prayers *(Acts 2:42)*.

4. *I reflect on what I have just read:*

One can never pray too much; rather, one can pray not enough.

Prayer is not a matter of words that one recites; it is an impulse toward God, an encounter with Him: a meeting in silence in order to listen to Him, to respond to Him, to praise Him, to thank Him, and to implore Him.

When one of His children begins to pray, God sets Himself to listening. To the Saint, Brother André Bessette, is attributed the saying: "God, who is all-good, is not far from you. He is near you. Each time you say the *Our Father*, He has His ear glued to your mouth."

Prayer always has its fruit. Its first fruit is the encounter with God. The

Gospel avows that, when we pray, God always gives us in return the Holy Spirit and His gifts. These gifts are needed for our living according to the Gospel and our tackling the problems that each day brings.

5. *I read some lines penned by John Paul II:*

What is prayer? It is generally considered a dialogue. In any conversation, there is always an "I" and a "you." In prayer, the "You" begins with a capital letter. The experience of prayer teaches us that, if initially the "I" seems the more important element, we eventually perceive that the reality is different: it is the "You" that is more important because our prayer has its origin in God. This is exactly what Saint Paul teaches us in the Letter to the Romans *(8:26)*. According to the Apostle, prayer is a reflex of all creation; therefore, in a certain sense, it has a cosmic function.

Man is the priest of creation, and he speaks for it in the measure that he is led by the Spirit. (*Mon livre de médi-*

tations, Éditions du Rocher, 2004, no. 548, p. 192.)

6. *I thank God as I say over and over:*

I give You thanks, Lord, for those who made You known to me and taught me to pray to You.

Then I implore Him more than once, saying:

Lord, teach me to pray better every day.

Teach me to be faithful to prayer.

7. *With Saint John Paul II and by his intercession, I present to God my personal intentions. I name the persons for whom I pray, and I tell God what I request of Him for them.*

8. *I pray for the Church and for all who live on earth:*

- I pray to You, Lord, that those baptized at an early age may from their youth learn how to encounter You in prayer.

- I pray to You that the religious, monks, and nuns, and all those in consecrated life may faithfully pray

to You every day for an extended
time.

- I ask that all the baptized may pray
  to You daily and that more numerous
  may be those who come together to
  pray to You at the Sunday Eucharist.

- That the heavens and the earth may
  sing Your praises, Lord.

- That the rich and poor, the Saints
  and sinners may invoke and bless
  You.

- That the sick may unite themselves
  to Your Son and offer to You with
  Him their sufferings.

- That Christians of every language
  and culture may give You thanks
  with one heart.

9. *I recite an* Our Father, *a* Hail Mary,
   and a Glory be.

LORD, TEACH ME TO LOVE

1. *I slowly make the Sign of the Cross while saying:* In the name of the Father, and of the Son, and of the Holy Spirit.

Then I say: Gracious God, help me to pray to You well with Saint John Paul II.

2. *I think about John Paul II:*

He wrote: "By the time I was twenty, I had already lost all those I loved and even those I could have loved, like my older sister about whom I learned that she had died six years before my birth. I had not reached the age of First Holy Communion when my mother died. . . ."

Despite these trials and all the others that he encountered in his life, John Paul II did not stop believing in love, and he applied himself to putting it into practice.

Jesus' teaching on love guided him.

3. *I read some verses from the New Testament:*

- God so loved the world that he gave his only Son, so that whoever believes in him might not perish but might have eternal life *(Jn 3:16)*.

- Jesus . . . having loved those who were his own in the world, loved them to the end *(Jn 13:1)*.

- I give you a new commandment: love one another. As I have loved you, love one another *(Jn 13:34)*.

- Whoever loves father or mother more than me is not worthy of me; and whoever loves son or daughter more than me is not worthy of me *(Mt 10:37)*.

- Whoever gives to one of these little ones even a cup of cold water . . . he shall not lose his reward *(Mt 10:42)*.

- If you love me, you will keep my commandments *(Jn 14:15)*.

4. *I reflect on what I have just read:*

To love is to have concern for others. It is to help others to live and to make strides toward happiness.

To love is to endeavor to put into practice the Golden Rule, which has been articulated in almost all religions and which Jesus enunciated thus: "You shall love your neighbor as yourself" *(Mt 22:39)*; or further: "Whatever you would want others to do to you, you should do for them" *(Mt 7:12)*.

It is impossible to attain to this while thinking only of oneself, being interested only in oneself.

It is impossible to reach this without thinking about one's neighbor with respect, affection, fairness, and compassion.

Love is opposed to indifference. It counters the slogan "Run for your life! Every man for himself!"

At some time or other, love meets the cross. Does the one who refuses to face suffering really know love? Does he know what great love is?

5. *I read some lines penned by John Paul II:*

The love which the Apostle Paul celebrates in the First Letter to the

Corinthians—the love which is "patient" and "kind" and "endures all things" *(1 Cor 13:4, 7)*—is certainly a demanding love. But this is precisely the source of its beauty: by the very fact that it is demanding, it builds up the true good of man and allows it to radiate to others. The good, says Saint Thomas, is by its nature "diffusive." Love is true when it creates the good of persons and of communities; it creates that good and gives it to others. Only the one who is able to be demanding with himself in the name of love can also demand love from others. Love is demanding. It makes demands in all human situations; it is even more demanding in the case of those who are open to the Gospel. Is this not what Christ proclaims in "His" commandment?

Today people need to rediscover this demanding love, for it is the truly firm foundation of the family, a foundation able to "endure all things." According to the Apostle, love is not able to "endure all things" if it yields to "jealousies" or if it is "boastful . . . arrogant or rude" *(see 1 Cor 13:4-5)*. True love, Saint Paul teaches, is different: "Love believes all things, hopes all things, endures all things" *(1 Cor 13:7)*. It is this love which "endures all things." At work within it is the power and strength of God Himself, who "is love" *(1 Jn 4:8, 16)*. At work within it is also the power and strength of Christ, the Redeemer of mankind and Savior of the world. (*Letter to families*, February 2, 1994, no. 14.)

6. *I thank God as I say over and over:*

For all the love that You have for me, Lord, I give You thanks.

Then I implore Him more than once, saying:

Teach me to love even as You love.

Teach me to love as Your Son Jesus loves all of us.

Teach me to love my neighbor as I myself like to be loved.

7. *With Saint John Paul II and by his intercession, I present to God my personal intentions. I name the persons*

for whom I pray, and I tell God what
I request of Him for them.

8. *I pray for the Church and for all who*
   live on earth:

- For those who are not loved—I pray
  to You for them, Lord.
- For those children who are rejected
  or abandoned—I pray for them.
- For those husbands and wives who
  promised one day to love one another
  forever and have not succeeded at
  doing so—I pray for them, Lord.
- For those who imagine that they
  love but really seek nothing other
  than their own satisfaction and happiness—I pray for them.
- For those who do not manage to
  love because they themselves were
  not loved—I pray to You for them.
- Come to the aid of all those who live
  without love, gracious God.
- Support those who strive to love in
  the midst of suffering.
- Open the eyes and hearts of those
  who scorn love.

9. *I recite an* Our Father, *a* Hail Mary, *and a* Glory be.

DAY NINE

LORD, TEACH ME TO FORGIVE

1. *I slowly make the Sign of the Cross while saying:* In the name of the Father, and of the Son, and of the Holy Spirit.

Then I say: Gracious God, help me to pray to You well with Saint John Paul II.

2. *I think about John Paul II:*

On May 13, 1981, he was the victim of an assassination attempt by Ali Agça, a right-wing Turkish militant. In 1983, he went to meet his would-be killer in an Italian prison and forgave him for this act of violence.

According to a United Press article, some years later John Paul II met with the mother and brother of Ali Agça.

John Paul II not only believed in the power of forgiveness, and he not only prayed daily "forgive us our trespasses as we forgive those who trespass against us," he also endeavored to put this prayer into practice.

3. *I read some verses from the New Testament:*

- Be kind to one another, compassionate, forgiving each other as God has forgiven you in Christ *(Eph 4:32)*.

- If your brother sins against you seven times a day, and turns to you seven times, and says, "I repent," you must forgive him *(Lk 17:4)*.

- Peter approaching asked him, "Lord, if my brother sins against me, how often must I forgive him? As often as seven times?" Jesus answered, "I say to you, not seven times but seventy-seven times" *(Mt 18:21-22)*.

- If you forgive others their failings, your Father in heaven will forgive you yours; but if you do not forgive others, neither will your Father forgive your failings *(Mt 6:14-15)*.

4. *I reflect on what I have just read:*

Forgiveness is the apex and finest flower of love. Whoever is not successful in forgiving others does not yet know how to love fully.

The forgiveness to which Jesus summons His disciples is wide and deep. It is disconcerting. This forgiveness extends not only to the people that we love, but also to those that we find difficult to love . . . and those who do not love us. It extends even to our enemies; this is something we often find impossible to do.

Without the power of the Holy Spirit, who can attempt to forgive his enemies?

Forgiveness is the source of life. It restarts and restores life—the life of the person who receives it and of the person who grants it.

It was on the Cross that Jesus made the most beautiful declaration of love, which was an avowal of forgiveness: "Father, forgive them, for they do not know what they are doing" *(Lk 23:34)*.

5. *I read some lines penned by John Paul II:*

Forgiveness is in no way opposed to justice, as if to forgive meant to overlook the need to right the wrong done.

It is rather the fullness of justice, leading to that tranquility of order which is much more than a fragile and temporary cessation of hostilities, involving as it does the deepest healing of the wounds which fester in human hearts. Justice and forgiveness are both essential to such healing.

Forgiveness is above all a personal choice, a decision of the heart to go against the instinct to pay back evil with evil. The measure of such a decision is the love of God who draws us to Himself in spite of our sin. It has its perfect exemplar in the forgiveness of Christ, Who on the Cross prayed: "Father, forgive them; for they know not what they do" *(Lk 23:34)*.

Forgiveness therefore has a divine source and criterion. This does not mean that its significance cannot also be grasped in the light of human reasoning; and this, in the first place, on the basis of what people experience when they do wrong. They experience their human weakness, and they want

others to deal leniently with them. Why
not therefore do toward others what we
want them to do toward us?

The ability to forgive lies at the
very basis of the idea of a future soci-
ety marked by justice and solidarity.
(*Message for the Celebration of the
World Day of Peace*, January 1, 2002.)

6. *I thank God as I say over and over:*

Thank You, Lord, for the many times
You have granted me Your forgiveness.

*Then I implore Him more than once,
saying:*

Teach me, Lord, to forgive others just
as I myself have been forgiven by You.

7. *With Saint John Paul II and by his
   intercession, I present to God my personal intentions. I name the persons
   for whom I pray, and I tell God what
   I request of Him for them.*

8. *I pray for the Church and for all who
   live on earth:*

• Forgive, Lord, the members of the
  Church who fail.

- Forgive, Lord, the leaders of the Church who do not always live what they preach.
- Change the hearts of those who refuse to forgive.
- Open the eyes of those who enrich themselves at the expense of the poor; change their hearts.
- Convert those who think that they can establish peace by doing violence; change their hearts.

I think of a person whom I find difficult to forgive, and I say:

- Lord, help me to forgive him/her.

I think of a person from whom I hope to receive forgiveness, and I say:

- Lord, move him/her to forgive me and help him/her to do it.

9. *I recite an* Our Father, *a* Hail Mary, *and a* Glory be.

A BRIEF CHRONOLOGY OF ST. JOHN PAUL II (1920–2014)

May 18, 1920

> Born as Karol Józef Wojtyla in Wadowice (Poland)

November 1, 1946

> Ordained a priest in Krakow

September 28, 1958

> Consecrated Auxiliary Bishop of Krakow, becoming the youngest Bishop in Poland

1962-1965

> Participated in the Second Vatican Council

January 13, 1964

> Named Archbishop of Krakow

June 26, 1967

> Created a Cardinal by Paul VI

October 16, 1978

> Elected the 264th Pope, at 58 years of age, on the eighth ballot. He took the name of John Paul II.

May 13, 1981
> Wounded in St. Peter's Square by a Turkish gunman, Ali Agça, whom he would later forgive and visit in prison

January 1, 1986
> Met the leaders of the Jewish community at the synagogue of Rome, the first time such an event took place

October 27, 1986
> Invited to Assisi the leaders of all ecclesial communities and various religions of the world for a time of joint prayer

April 2, 2005
> Died at 9:37 p.m. in his apartment at the Vatican

May 1, 2011
> Declared "Blessed" by Pope Benedict XVI

April 27, 2014
> Canonized by Pope Francis

SOME FEATURES OF HIS PONTIFICATE

- His pontificate lasted 26 years, the third longest in the history of the Church.

- He was the first non-Italian Pope in 455 years, that is, since the pontificate of the Dutchman Adrian VI.

- He was the first Polish Pope in Church history and the first Pope to visit a communist country (Poland).

- He initiated the first international, interreligious gathering of Assisi (1984), which brought together 194 religious leaders.

- He traveled through 129 nations during his pontificate.

- He was a great defender of human rights.

- He was the originator of the World Youth Days.

- He beatified 1,340 persons and canonized 483.

SOME DOCUMENTS OF
HIS PONTIFICATE

HIS ENCYCLICALS

A N encyclical is a particularly important and solemn letter which the Pope addresses to all Catholics and in which he treats questions regarding faith or morals or pastoral matters. Encyclicals are designated by the first words in their original, Latin text; for example, *Redemptor Hominis* because it begins with the words "The Redeemer of man. . . ."

John Paul published fourteen encyclicals:

March 4, 1979

> *Redemptor Hominis* (The Redeemer of Man): places Christ at the center of the universe, humankind, and history

November 30, 1980

> *Dives in Misericordia* (Rich in Mercy): about the mercy of God the Father

September 14, 1981

> *Laborem Exercens* (Doing Work): about human work

June 2, 1985

> *Slavorum Apostoli* (Apostles of the Slavs): about Saints Cyril and Methodius on the occasion of the eleventh centenary of their work of evangelization

May 18, 1986

> *Dominum et Vivificantem* (Lord and Giver of Life): about the role of the Holy Spirit in the life of the Church and the world

March 25, 1987

> *Redemptoris Mater* (The Mother of the Redeemer): about the Virgin Mary

December 30, 1987

> *Sollicitudo Rei Socialis* (Concern for Social Matters): about social issues

December 7, 1990

> *Redemptoris Missio* (Mission of the

Redeemer): about the missionary activity of the Church

May 1, 1991

Centesimus Annus (Hundredth Year): about the social teaching of the Church on the occasion of the hundredth anniversary of the encyclical *Rerum Novarum* (Of new things)

August 6, 1993

Veritatis Splendor (Splendor of the Truth): about the moral teaching of the Church

March 25, 1995

Evangelium Vitæ (The Gospel of Life): about the inviolable character of human life

May 25, 1995

Ut Unum Sint (That They May Be One): about Christian unity

September 14, 1998

Fides et Ratio (Faith and Reason): about the relationship between faith and reason

April 17, 2003

Ecclesia de Eucharistia (The Church Lives by the Eucharist); about the importance of the Eucharist in the life of the Church